A Pocket Pierre Workbook

Unblocking

Removing Blocks to Understanding

By

Pierre Grimes

...an adaptation of *To Artemis*
by Pierre Grimes

Contents

Unblocking

Removing Blocks to Understanding: Doing Philosophical Midwifery for Yourself

Introduction

Carved above the entrance to the Temple at Delphi in Greece are the words, "Know Thyself." This is a simple, direct, complete statement, full of mystery, that has lasted through the centuries. This workbook gives you the tools to meet the challenge of that phrase, Know Thyself, using the art of Philosophical Midwifery. This is a Socratic art because in helping people bring to birth ideas they are pregnant with, we are functioning like a midwife.

But why return to these ancients? Is there not enough in our present day to help us through our problems and difficulties? Sadly, our age is lacking in what was once the strength of the ancients.

Those living in the past classical age had access to a wide body of works that could help them understand themselves. In the modern world, these works are only studied as literature and no longer as methods for self-discovery. Homer's works, the *Iliad* and the *Odyssey,* were common sources for insights into oneself, and along with Homer's works, there was a vital and challenging philosophy of the Platonic and Hellenic tradition. I explored this idea in depth in "Homer and the Struggle for Excellence," (www.noeticsociety.org).

This workbook has evolved from the many years I have pondered over my own difficulties as well as reflecting on the dialogues I have had with others. It is an adaptation of a more in-depth work of self-discovery, *To Artemis,* that is available from www.academyofplatonicstudies.com. The original *To Artemis* program was presented as a HyperCard-compatible stack for the Macintosh computer in 1988, and later it was freely offered at www.openingmind.com. Should you review it, you will find it structured as an ongoing dialogue that allows answers to be directly typed into the program. This present version has been revised and adapted. Joseph Grimes contributed greatly to this version as well as the early version, and Cathy Wilson and Nancy Grimes also contributed to this revised version.

Philosophical Midwifery and Psychology

In our age, people look to psychology for insights into themselves. However, there is a vast difference between today's popular psychology and what is in those classical works. The ancients sought to understand themselves through the study of the mind; they sought to use the mind to study the mind. They saw that the self is no different than mind itself.

Psychologists want to change behavior, but whether or not they are able to achieve the more profound goals of self-discovery is quite another thing. Equally, contemporary religions focus on sin and guilt as their central and basic problem and not a path of self-discovery. Returning to this classical way of self-reflection will revive a more profound way of understanding oneself, different than what is offered through psychology and religion.

The block to our understanding ourselves is simply that we are not aware of deeply-held beliefs about ourselves that create our difficulties. It is not that these beliefs are unconscious, but rather that we assume them to be so true that we don't even talk about them. Since these beliefs are for the most part unspoken or unsuspected, we are not aware of the role they play in blocking the goals we have set for ourselves. These beliefs are at odds with achieving the goals we most want. They are, in principle, irreconcilable with who we would be if we were to achieve those goals. The result? We experience all kinds of blocks to getting what we most want—and we do not understand why we are blocked. What is this thing that blocks us? In Philosophical Midwifery, we call it "having a problem." It is some belief about ourselves and about our reality, a belief which is genuinely false; it is a sick belief, so we call it a pathologos.

You can learn more about the pathologos in the companion volume, *The Pocket Pierre,* Grimes and Wilson, 2013; find it on Amazon.

For a more in-depth exploration of the method and its history and implications, see *Philosophical Midwifery: A New Paradigm for Understanding Human Problems with its Validation* by Pierre Grimes and Regina L. Uliana, available on Amazon and from www.noeticsociety.org.

The pathologos, the sick belief, is not something you can call a sin, nor is it some psychological instinctive force we have to learn to deal with. It is something we learned in our youth and now we apply it to situations that seem to us to be equivalent, but they are not the same, only similar.

Let's put it in another way. A personal problem then is something that blocks us from achieving our personally meaningful goals. It is something we learned in our youth and we unknowingly apply it to a present circumstance. What you learned in the past to help you through difficulties, you are applying to situations that are different, and so it doesn't work.

We must uncover these unsuspected beliefs by:

- discovering their origin;

- recognizing their power and influence in our lives;

- learning how these beliefs function in our present;

- and then testing our newly discovered understanding in those situations that previously gave us such difficulties.

This is the path of self-discovery. It is the path of the ancients and it will return us to our own golden age, just as it once did to those living in the Hellenic age.

The Direct Path:
Striving for Excellence

You can most easily discover these beliefs by focusing on your *personally meaningful goals*. Your goal can be in any area of your life, such as relationships, school, business, athletics, or finances, as long as it is personally meaningful to you. When we pursue our personal goals, that's when obstacles get in our way. Our pathologos beliefs are forced into view as we attempt to gain those meaningful goals. The more significant the goal, the more clearly they show up. Thus the most direct way to bring the false beliefs to the surface is to pursue our most meaningful goals. This is the path of excellence, doing your best in pursuing your most personally meaningful goal, you "go for broke," you throw everything into the struggle, and so it becomes a spiritual goal.

This idea of excellence is most important. Why? Because when we work without excellence, we escape seeing ourselves and our problems. To accomplish our goals in a lesser way is to lose the chance to face and uncover our problems. When this happens, it's evidence of a problem. When we pursue our personal goals (and reflect on them), we can see ourselves and our problems more clearly, so we gain the clearest insight and understanding into ourselves. Thus we need to actively seek to reflect upon our lives and begin the quest to "Know Thyself."

The very process of *doing* and *reflecting* is the way to change. Making a commitment, then taking the time and energy to answer the following questions, and then reflecting on these answers, is the key to understanding and growth. We need to *do*....that is the reason we call this a *work*book. To discover yourself and grow personally in a meaningful way, YOU must do something. No one can do it for you, but then no one else can take that growth away from you, either.

People often ask how they can do this work for themselves, especially since they may not know anyone who is a philosophical midwife. We have designed this workbook to give you the tools you will need to undertake the work for yourself.

Signs of a Problem

Experiencing obstacles and difficulties in life is not, by itself, a sufficient sign of having a problem. Before we can say we have a problem, we must commit ourselves in some way to a personally significant goal and observe the obstacles we experience which block our efforts to reach that goal. In this way, the signs of having a problem must include one or more of the following. Please check which one(s) may apply to you:

- Not striving for your most personally meaningful ideals and goals;
- Failure to adequately study and prepare to achieve your goals;
- Setting secondary goals as if they were primary goals;
- Making the practical issues the only significant ones;

- Letting opportunities go by;
- Sabotaging opportunities for success;
- Loss of concentration;
- Inability to resist distractions and tangents;
- Accepting, believing, making up excuses and/or convincing others that you are not responsible;
- Functioning ideally in crises, either alone or with others, but expressing stress or anxiety before and after such events;
- Engaging in destructive behaviors, especially when you are close to achievement.

The Pathologos is Not a Sin

It is important to remember that a problem is not a sin or some kind of neurosis or something to feel guilt or vengeance about; rather, it is something to learn from and to become better by reflecting upon it. As strange as it may seem, a problem is actually a false belief about ourselves and our reality that we cling to for reasons we do not understand, and these beliefs are inconsistent with our most meaningful and personal goals.

As you have seen, we call such a false belief a sick belief, or pathologos.

Remember that a pathologos problem blocks our growth and confuses us, because while we are awake and alert, we can't see why we are again in a situation we previously promised ourselves to avoid. Thus a problem is much like being asleep while awake: asleep to the nature of the problem, awake to each of the parts without being aware of the unity that binds them together. Therefore, a pathologos becomes a pattern that plays itself out again and again in your life, a series of events linked together that plays out its consequences in our lives over and over. We see and feel each event, but we fail to recognize its structure, yet its force is destructive and makes emotional shambles of our lives. Therefore, our first effort must be to make all the parts visible, link all the parts into a whole, and see the bond that connects them.

Also remember that the cause of our problems is always from something we learned from early past scenes, though we did not even suspect it. We unknowingly became believers of a false belief about ourselves. We thought the authorities in our life—usually our parents—really knew the truth about us and about reality. To discover such false beliefs and undo this false learning is the path of discovering who and what you are.

Understanding the Workbook

This workbook is designed to be an aid in the process of self-discovery, to help you to identify, understand, and resolve the problems that hold you back. Resolving these problems can bring you growth, understanding, achievement, excellence – and a growing measure of peace and happiness.

Recently, there has been an explosion of "self-help" books and seminars. What makes this workbook different? It is based on doing and reflecting, with *you* as an active participant. This is more than just reading or listening to recordings - a very significant difference. Merely reading or just listening will not substantially change anything in your life, just like watching TV is not living life and reading about jogging is not jogging.

By participating in the *doing*, you will also come to recognize that you are awakening your understanding to a higher and different level. This will help you see the truthfulness behind words, to see the way they form patterns that shape our experience and mold our understanding around it. Appreciating words, being sensitive to them, is what we call *seeing into the self.*

The level you reach will depend on how sincerely you take on the task of self-analysis, as well as how much tension you can endure as you proceed.

You may either skip among the sections or proceed straight through the workbook. We have designed this workbook to accommodate both styles. If you have a paper copy of this book, you can write in it, doodle in it, copy pages for yourself, and more. If you are reading this digitally, you can make notes in your e-reader. In either case, perhaps you will want to buy or make a blank journal (call it your PM Journal) to respond to the questions at length. A good tutorial for easily making your own book can be found at http://tinyurl.com/blankbook .

It will be helpful for you to record your thoughts, feelings, states of mind and ideas while going through this workbook. You will likely have many spontaneous reflections, thoughts, and insights during this exploration and you will want to preserve them for later reflection. If later you recall other areas of your life where you have experienced your problem, please note them in your journal and include them in your analysis. In this way, you will build a resource to reflect upon later.

Please don't be in a rush to complete this work. Take your time and reflect on the puzzles, the insights, and the understandings that you come to. Do not be concerned how much you write in each section. Write just enough to express your thoughts, feelings, and insights. Take the time to breathe; relax into yourself and become a friend to yourself, and enjoy the journey.

People who have completed this workbook say that they have a tremendous feeling of relief ... like the weight of the world has been lifted off their shoulders. They say that they experience a pleasant euphoria and a feeling of ease and freedom.

If for any reason you should decide to withdraw from your search, the workbook will remain as something to return to at a later date. When you do resume the challenge, it will certainly be significant to be aware of the factors that caused both your withdrawal and your return.

The next section is the *doing* part of the book. It will guide you on the journey of self-discovery by bringing you to new levels of insight using both questions and reflections, and the questions you answer will bring you to reflect upon yourself in a most thoughtful way.

Before going into the *doing* section of the book I have included *Questions We Are Often Asked*. We hope it helps you to more fully understand the workbook and this method.

Exploring with Others

While the questions have been designed for an inner dialogue, they can easily be used in a dialogue with someone else. Often you see much more when you share with another person. When you explore using these questions, keep a record of your reflections: write down the answers in a journal, because by returning to it again and again, you will see so much more. It is as if there is too much to see all at once, and so by returning and reflecting on it, you are able to see the patterns and make connections so necessary for insights and understanding. It is only by repeated reflection and wondering that we can reach the truth about ourselves through understanding.

Questions We Are Often Asked

As we developed this workbook, people often asked the same kinds of questions. We're including (and answering) them here.

How can I tell if I need to use this workbook?

If you want to understand yourself more fully and grow, if you want to understand why you experience difficulties that hinder, block, or turn you away from achieving your practical and personally meaningful goals, then this workbook is for you. If you struggle with harmful personal behaviors that stop you from becoming your best self, this workbook is for you. In following the practices here, you will explore ideas in a new way, and it is this new way of approaching human problems that will bring you to a profound way of understanding. In grasping this way of understanding you will see how you can apply it in many new and exciting ways.

How do the questions work?

These questions can be answered either briefly or in some depth. Consider these questions to be from someone you trust, who is only interested in helping you understand yourself.

The questions will bring to the surface the very way you have understood your life, and you will see very clearly what it will mean for you to keep doing your life the way you have, with your current understanding. This understanding has created a model that you continuously reflect upon, even though you may not be aware of it. This model has shaped what we call our past, present, and future. Our questions are designed to surface those distortions and take away their influence.

Will I find something fearful in my past?

Probably not. Instead, you will discover that what is responsible for your problems are not monstrous things from your past, but simple ideas that you inferred from simple scenes.

If I just answer questions, how can I learn anything about myself that I don't already know?

You already know, but you keep forgetting. The dialogue helps to bring up to the surface, in a rational manner, what you already know. Then, by reflecting again and again on what you said, you begin to make connections. This clarifies the themes that have caused you trouble in your life. This process helps you to remember and understand.

But WHY do you have to challenge beliefs?

Suppose, for a moment, that you discover yourself running into the same kind of problems again and

again—whether in your studies, your work, or your relations with others. When you strive to achieve those things which are most important to you, suppose that you experience these problems even more intensely.

Again, suppose you discover that behind those obstacles and difficulties are nothing more than beliefs you hold about yourself, your self-image. Would you be curious about those beliefs and want to know about them and how you came to learn them? And also, why it is that they seem to gain intensity whenever you pursue your most significant goals?

This workbook guides you through reflections and recollections to discover the answers to these very questions. As these things become clear to you, you will grasp that as long as these beliefs are not challenged and not exposed, they will continue to block you from attaining you noblest goals.

So the workbook brings about insights into how you understand yourself, right?

Yes, and as you become familiar with the process, you will discover that it provides you with a new model of understanding, as well as a way of understanding yourself and others.

Are you saying that this workbook is the ONLY way to understand yourself?

Not at all. We seek to know ourselves in many ways, and certainly not all use the same approach. But when you use this workbook to understand yourself, you will be gaining insights into the process that generates beliefs, and you will learn about the kind of problems that are generated from beliefs.

Since this workbook is not interactive, how can it possibly "know" about my problems?

The questions proceed the way a dialogue should proceed—step by step to a natural conclusion. This is possible because it follows the very way in which problems come into existence. By charting out the forces that maintain the problems, we can challenge their right to exist. This workbook surfaces the false ideas which play a role in our lives, ideas that we have never examined or put into words. Then, once we recognize the role these false ideas play, they lose their ruinous power.

But this workbook sounds like psychology. Is it?

This workbook is not psychology because it simply explores the nature of false beliefs and inquires into why we believed them. Thus we discover that we are not driven by some instinct, some unconscious desire, or some biological or emotional force; rather we have kept believing those false beliefs because there appeared to be good reason to conclude the way we did. When these false beliefs are exposed as false, we realize how they have affected us, and we will reject them. This workbook is your practical application of Philosophical Midwifery.

How long does it usually take to complete an exploration of a problem?

While it may be possible for some people to go through the workbook in an evening or two, most people take longer, allowing plenty of time for reflecting and going over their answers. Thus, some people require only a few days, while some require several months. This also depends on individual ways of working, time available, the amount of tension created and tolerated.

You'll find there is a difference between going through the workbook and resolving a problem. There are many aspects to a problem, and you will need to look at it from several perspectives. Some may be relatively easy, while some are rather hard. Take the time you need to work through the problem.

Isn't it possible to reach wrong conclusions and misjudge others and ourselves?

Yes, that is true; however, this work is about purifying your understanding. Consider: whatever understanding you reach will be tested or tempered in the fire of your own experience, because we enter again and again into problem scenes, so puzzling over their meanings will give us clearer understanding. The power and intensity of a problem diminishes in this process, and as you will doubtless find, it is never without its most interesting surprises.

Caution

As you proceed through this workbook, try to maintain a spirit of fairness and sincerity in your explorations and avoid any hint of the methods and style of an attorney cross-examining a witness. Further, remember that your purpose is not to assign blame and guilt. Those who contributed to your problem certainly had no idea of what was being learned. Surely this is obvious, for in all families, there are moments of love, much is sacrificed, and all parents dream that their children might be enriched by their successes and spared learning their faults; they take no pleasure in learning just how short-lived their dream was. Therefore, it is better for us to accept our challenges and bring an end to what has limited both our understanding and our vision, without blaming.

CONGRATULATIONS for accepting this challenge!

It is no frivolous game you are undertaking, but one that is as difficult as it is rewarding. So make the commitment, understand yourself, and grow.

"Within every problem there is a gift for you in its hands.
You seek these problems because you need their gifts."

Richard Bach, *Illusions*

"You! You are a man! You have a Voice!
Speak your mind, for meaningful sounds
have been awaited since immeasurable time.
And, through continual questioning and reflection,
may you polish to a brilliance that
which illuminates the soul and so
ends the dark silence of the ages."

My comrade, Posa, who died in combat in WWII

Part One:
A Goal and the Problem

A goal is not a dream wish.
If you say you have a goal
but can't describe the stages
you have to go through to get it,
then it's a dream wish.
But if you can describe the steps
or the stages
you have to go through
to achieve it, then it's a goal.
If the steps to reach the goal
are well known to you and
the way to secure each step is clear to you,
then if you encounter any difficulty
securing your goal you will know
just where you are stuck and
it is there that your problem shows itself.

We make goals for ourselves anytime we desire to do our best at anything. Driving a car perfectly, writing a report or a letter that expresses yourself most sincerely, doing some household chore most perfectly, or even when engaged in a talk—so long as you want to express yourself most honestly and sincerely. But in this process, a goal must have stages you go through, steps that require planning, reflection, and understanding to accomplish. If a goal has these characteristics, then we can see where a problem emerges. What is most interesting about a problem is that it can show itself in different ways in several of these stages!

What is a Problem?

We call a problem anything that happened to turn you away from your goal—anything that delayed it, anything that diluted it, and anything that led you to give up your goal.

Now that you have reflected on this idea of a goal, would you please identify one or more goals that you consider to be personally meaningful to you.

What comes to your mind as you reflect on the problems that you have encountered in pursuing those goals you just listed? Provide details so that you can reflect on their sameness and differences.

Is it likely that unless you resolve these problems, you are likely to encounter some of the same problems when you seek, once again, to achieve your higher goals?

Consider, isn't it likely that completing this workbook would count as one of your goals?

What do you imagine you will learn about yourself if you decide to do your best completing this workbook—that is, with excellence?

Excellence

When setting your goals you knew, of course, that you would encounter difficulties. You also knew the goals would be worth the effort otherwise you never would have set those goals and faced those difficulties. What you wanted was to gain that goal, the whole of it, and that means doing it right.

Do you agree that to achieve any goal, but to do so without achieving it with the degree of excellence you most desire, leaves you in a position of not fully mastering your goal?

Wouldn't it be interesting to be able to do your best in the best manner possible, and to bring that spirit, or sense of excellence into other aspects of your life?

In what area of your life would it be most significant for you to achieve this thing we are calling excellence?

Is it possible that if you were to take this workbook as a personal challenge you could surface an aspect of your problem which otherwise you might have ignored?

What does it mean if you have been able to achieve success in what you do but have not achieved it with excellence? Do the goals which you have pursued require you to ignore your higher goals and settle for less? In what way(s)?

Is it possible that your successes have nothing to do with your achieving excellence? What does that mean?

Time to Reflect

You may be feeling a little overwhelmed right now and curious as to where this workbook is going.

For this reason, we have supplied a chart outlining where you are in the process. Please take the time to review it. We want to help you understand this process and feel comfortable with proceeding. You have just finished Part One.

Part One	A Goal and the Problem
Part Two	**Revealing the Problem**
Part Three	**Uncovering the Past**
Part Four	**Reflecting on the Past**
Part Five	**Questioning What Has Been Discovered**
Part Six	**Power of Silence and Power of Words**
Part Seven	**Knowing and Convincing**
Part Eight	**Taking the Challenge**
Part Nine	**Self Discovery**
Part Ten	**Higher Goals**

Part Two:
Revealing the Problem

Statement of the Problem

How might you explain not fully achieving your goal with excellence? Try to express as best you can the reasons you give yourself for this failure. Find the words that can best express it. This explanation will be your *Statement of the Problem.*

Is there an attitude or an image that seems to accompany your explanation, adding an emotional aspect to it? Please add it to your statement.

As you give this account is there a sense that you are scolding yourself, blaming yourself, condemning yourself—or others? Try to describe this "sense" and consider it as an addition to your problem statement. Note: It is important to write these "scolding" and "blaming" remarks down with as much accuracy as you can.

Again, as you give this account, is there some tension you experience? If so, where in your body do you experience it?

What is it like? Would you please describe it?

Have you felt this sensation before? When? Describe it. Perhaps it is a common experience when you experience tension.

Please describe when you most recently experienced your problem. It is likely it was an event that had an interesting or unique beginning, so please add as much detail as possible. Again, make sure you describe anyone who was present and note their response to what was going on. Since the event had an ending, would you describe the effect that had on you. What state of mind, or feelings, did you go through? Describe what thoughts and images you experienced.

Scenes

Please note: A problem is an event that goes through stages and has scenes, much like in a drama, where certain prescribed roles play themselves out.

The Scenes within Your Problem-Event

Now let us explore the problem you just described in more detail. The problem-event you have selected probably has several scenes in it to which you can apply this analysis. However, even if the problem you are working on doesn't have a number of scenes, you will still find it important to answer these questions. Later, when you explore your other problems, it is likely that they will have a sufficient number of scenes for you to gain additional insights into by going through this analysis.

As you reflect upon it now, in what way would you say that it could have been possible to experience some of the first few scenes in this event without having to go through all the rest?

As you examine each of these scenes, in what way would you say that some of the scenes that come later seem to be connected?

Now, please recall the most negative scene, when you felt the worst, and try to explain how the scenes that follow (after this negative scene) seem to fit together—or are in some way connected in a sequence.

If you can identify the scene that started this sequence, then you have identified the "turning point" scene. Consider, if you have identified that scene, in what way is it likely that the scenes that follow have a momentum of their own? Please describe that experience as best you can.

As you reflect on the scenes of this problem-event would you say that there was a certain momentum it had, pulling you into it and keeping you there? If so, please explain what it was like to experience that sense of the "momentum." What was it like to be "kept there"?

The Doorway into the Problem

We call that turning point scene the pivotal scene. We refer to it as "The Doorway into the Problem."

Once you reached that doorway, is it not likely that you were "locked in," as it were? Please explain your reaction to being "locked in."

Could you say, then, that when you go through the doorway you are no longer in control and that the momentum of the problem carries you on through it? Describe this sense of not being in control.

Study the scenes you have just described, reflect on each, and consider something quite curious: in what way can you say that not only are you "locked in" and experience a sense of some force, or momentum, carrying you along, but that you also seem to be ignoring the fact that you have done this before? Is this state one in which you can easily forget what you know—and so act in a state of forgetfulness?

Obstacles

Anything that blocks you from achieving any of the steps or stages of your goals of personal excellence we call "Obstacles." They constitute the elements of your problem. When you solve the problem, the obstacles are resolved.

Make Notes in your Journal

Now, in going through this very section, you are surfacing states of mind that are similar to what you experience in your problem-state. Watch carefully as they emerge; make notes in your journal of the thoughts, moods, and states of mind you experience as you go through this workbook.

Be watchful for the patterns that may be becoming familiar to you.

Ready to Quit?

Notice all tangents, urges to postpone, voices that argue you have done enough and should now rest, and moods that dampen your enthusiasm for this effort.

Keep a separate log of them in your journal. You can see the problems you encounter while doing this work as another manifestation of your problem.

Interrelationship among Problems

It is very likely that if you explore several problems, you will find that those problems are interrelated. Sooner or later, you will relate any and all difficulties to a single and fundamental problem, which forms the fabric of our pathologos.

Now, please review your description and make sure you have included how you felt in each scene, as well as what was said by each of the parties involved.

Have you described how each of the persons looked or appeared in each of these scenes?

Analysis of a Single Scene

It is possible that you have recollected a problem with only one scene in it, for, indeed, there are problems that seem to spring from only one scene. If this is the case, as you proceed, you will notice that through the following questions you may recollect other details and, perhaps, additional scenes which have been forgotten. Therefore, if you have such a scene, go ahead and sketch it (or paint it) and make it the object of your reflections. Don't worry about whether or not it has artistic value, because simply in doing this you will discover much that is significant and personally meaningful. As you recall more details of that scene add them to your sketch or painting.

The High and the Low

As you consider each of these scenes, please identify when you would say you were high, or in a positive state.

In the same way, identify when you felt most down, depressed, or in a negative state.

Negative State of Mind

When you reflect on your experiences, some states of mind or feelings may be called "negative" because you don't like being in them or going through them. It may be a state that you want to be out of, that you would love to end, or perhaps it is a state that hangs over you like a cloud—that state we call a "negative state of mind."

Example of diagramming a problem

Now it is time to diagram this event of your problem to show the dynamics of the problem you went through. This is done by describing each of the scenes that your problem went through and indicating within each scene the actions, words, and feelings of the persons involved.

We shall offer an example of a problem so that you can see how it is done. This problem was the author's problem and we are using it here an example of charting the problem.

The Problem

I play out my mother's role and can't stop being confrontive, so I lose another friend!

1

A friend invites me to his house. He is with his wife. He invites me to read a proposal he has written.
The atmosphere is very "matter-of-fact."

2

I read it and say, "It's no good. There is nothing good in it." He is humiliated in front of his wife. I am presenting a matter-of-fact appearance.

3

I present myself as uncompromising and not giving an inch. He is taken aback and asks what I mean.

4

I tell him, "It's bullshit! There's nothing in it. It's nothing but empty rhetoric." My words are final, matter-of-fact.

5

I don't offer to help him make it better. I dismiss him. My attitude is justified and not offering any possibility for discussion. That ends our relationship of many years.

6

Later, there is an opportunity to apologize and make it better, but I leave it as it is. But I miss his friendship. I was surprised to find out later that he thought of me as a friend.

Looking for Patterns

Now consider, you have just described a sequence of events and it includes actions and attitudes. Would you say you are seeing that a pattern this sequence repeats itself?

Do you see a pattern that seems to carry you along with it and which appears to have a momentum of its own? Please explain.

Your workbook exploration will bring you to understand why these particular patterns occur when they do and the significance of their necessity, but before you reach that point, there is more for you to explore.

Part Three:
Uncovering the Past

Recent Experiences of that State of Mind

As you reflect on the past few years of your life, can you recall situations where you experienced states of mind similar to those you just described—states of mind in the problem—at work, at home, or perhaps with family, friends, neighbors or others?

Please list some of these situations and then briefly describe:

How did you feel?

How did you believe you may have appeared to those with whom you were relating?

How did you feel about appearing that way?

Recall what you said to yourself after this experience.

What do you find common among these situations?

What effect did these states of mind have on these situations?

Consider, why do you think that these states of mind have played such a significant role in your life?

Similar States in Your More Distant Past

As you reflect on the problems as well as the state of mind you just described, would you say you experienced similar states of mind in your past—especially in your early years when you were living with your parents or with those who raised you?

Take a few minutes to recall that past episode. Recall as much detail as you can.

The Problem-Event in Childhood

Now that you have identified a problem-event from your past, it will be necessary to ask you some questions about it that are very similar to those you answered before.

Describe the situation in which the problem occurred.

How old were you?

Where did the event take place?

Did it occur outdoors?

In a house? In your home?

What room (or rooms) did it occur in?

Who was present? Please include everyone—even those in the background.

If at some later time, you recall another past event that was either as intense or more intense than the one you just described, make an analysis of it.

Intensity

There are some people who cannot recall an occasion where they experienced that "intense" state of mind—or they have difficulty doing so. Consider it may be that it was a state of mind that was always present in your early years and to single out one occasion may be difficult. In that case, reflect and recall any occasion when that state was present and use that scene for your exploration.

If you still experience difficulty in recalling scenes and cannot come up with any, just consider that you are encountering an obstacle along the way to your goal. This can happen at any stage of the philosophical analysis, even during the making of conclusions. When it occurs, just describe your present state of mind and note what you are going through as you confront this obstacle. Then treat it as you would another problem. Repeat this process until you can resume your former analysis.

Participants in that Past Problem

Consider the people who were included in this past problem-event.

Did you know some of these people very well?

Family members and other authorities could have been there. Identify each person by name and/or their relationship with you.

As you do this, do you notice that these are the people you depended upon for guidance, support, and for your survival?

Consider, were there any alternatives other than learning how to endure or "put up with" the situation you found yourself in?

What do you imagine would have happened had you rejected as false all that was happening in that problem-event?

Again, what if you had opposed what was going on?

And what if you said what you wanted to say or ask at that time?

Reviewing before Diagramming

Now, after reviewing your description of the past event, consider whether you can add to your account:

How did you feel during each scene?

How did those who were most active in playing out this scene appear to you?

Did you receive all their attention, all their concern, at this time?

As you consider this event would you say that this was an unusual, if not rare, performance they were playing out?

Since you were receiving all their care, attention, and focus, does this scene communicate to you that they care? That you exist? That you are someone worthy of such a display? Please put into words what you are thinking.

Did those who played out this scene appear as sincere, as if they truly know what is good and bad, right and wrong? Is it possible you have appeared that way to others?

If you have appeared in the way you experienced this past event, are you playing out anything you learned from this "game?" What?

Is having a problem imitating these past scenes, only you are choosing to play one role rather than the other role?

What does that mean to you, now?

Again, please be careful to note how you felt and how each person appeared to you.

Was anyone missing from the scene who could have changed the outcome if they had been there? Did any of those who were present play an observer role? If so what does that mean?

As you consider each of these scenes, at what point in the problem-event would you say you felt most "down" (or in a negative state) and at what point did you feel most positive?

And, in a similar way, describe the states of mind of each of the others who were in those scenes (whether they were active or passive).

Diagramming Your Past Event

Recall how you described and modeled your present problem and using that as a model, please describe this past event. Please include a date of the event and your approximate age.

Note that for nearly every scene you can include an action taking place, the words or thoughts that are occurring, and your state of mind, or what you are feeling.

As a way of illustrating this process, take a look at the following diagram.

The author was twelve years old when the following event took place. It relates to the example problem of his that was diagrammed earlier in Part Two.

1

A new friend persuades me to play hooky with him and my mother finds out. I am feeling doomed. She looks hard, determined and very angry. I say nothing.

2

My mother takes me to my friend's house and knocks on the door. Standing in front of the friend's mother. Feeling doomed. No words.

3

Feeling: Emptiness and futility. My mother issues a severe warning to my friend's mother: "I don't want your son to play with mine. He is no good and will be a bad influence on your boy."

4

I say nothing and feel humiliated. Mother says: "My son is no good!" She is sad, matter-of-fact, sure and her words are final. I think, "It doesn't matter what I think or say."

5

We return home and nothing more is said. Later, my mother answers the phone. She says, "Your friend asks if you can go with him and his family for a drive in the country." I say nothing.

6

Mother looks at me—waiting for an answer. I say no. It ends my relationship with my friend, never to see him again. I have no feelings. I walk away.

THE PROBLEM:

I keep getting close to what I want and feel I won't get it and it won't be real anyway. It is better not to achieve. Everyone is disillusioned and ends up disappointed.

Following, you will find a blank diagram to use in your own explorations.

As you review your diagram, please see if in each scene you have noted three things, for in each scene there was an action taking place, some words or thoughts that were known to you, and there must have been some state of mind present, or attitude, or feelings displayed. Have you included them in your diagram?

Please feel free to make copies of the diagram to use with problems as they emerge.

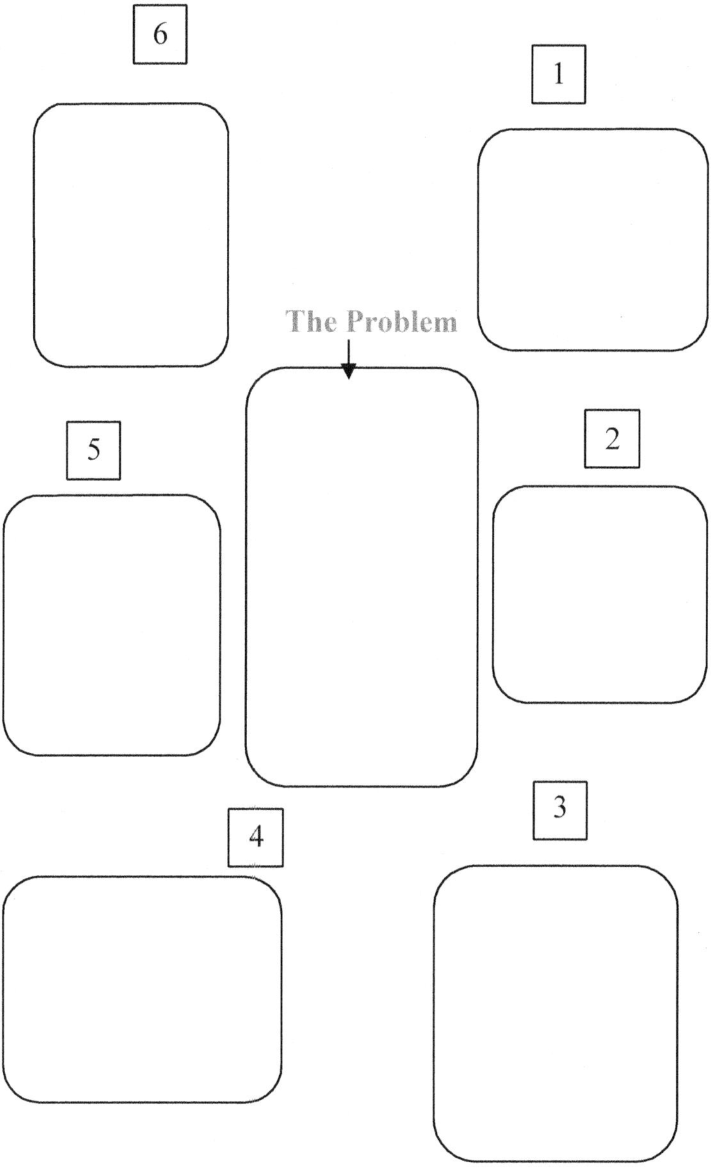
6
1
The Problem
5
2
4
3

Part Four:
Reflecting on the Past

Reviewing the Language

Please compare your description of the present event and past event. Note the language used to describe each event, past and present.

Note the similarities and differences in language between them.

Be attentive to similar experiences, ideas, and images. You may want to use your journal for these reflections.

Review the way the negative and positive states appear in the present and past events. Be attentive to something curious: What if the positive and more intense states of mind are linked to your experiencing the negative states of mind? Just what would that mean? What if you can't have that intense state of mind without the negative?

Then you could treat your high, or intense state, as another problem; you could go through the questions and make a study of the influence of this high state of mind on your life.

But then, if these states of mind are linked together, how can you get the good alone and by itself?

Looking at Your Language

Now, please reflect on your present problem-event and compare it with your statement of the past problem-event.

How many parallels can you notice between this past problem and the problem scenes you reported in your present circumstances? Please describe those that you found most interesting.

What similarities do you find in the language you used, in the expressions, and in your choice of words?

Are there also similarities between the problem-events as well as between their scenes?

As you examine this material, could you say your problem statement can apply to both the past and present, or would you say it fits better with the past? Do you see more interesting similarities between the statement of the problem in reference to the past or the present?

Consider this: HOW does the statement of your present problem set you up to deal with the present AS IF it were your past?

But if the problem statement fits with the past better than the present, then it may be that you are anticipating your present situations in terms of your past, or could you say that you are living the present as if it were your past?

If so, how can you get out of your past and live in the present?

Now, would you agree that this is indeed curious? Why would you be anticipating the present problem difficulties in terms of an incident that you experienced many years ago?

Reflections: the Past Problem

Could you say that through this past problem-event those who were present were showing what really mattered to them?

Were they not showing that they cared about something?

...cared enough to show you—or let you know about—what mattered most to them?

What, then, would you say that this means? For this event was important for them too, wasn't it?

They revealed themselves, through this event, didn't they? What did they reveal? Their values? Their fundamental beliefs? Please explain.

To reveal themselves in this way, didn't they have to break out of their everyday way of being?

Then, in breaking out of their "everyday way of being," the problem-event is special and significant.

But are these problem-events ways of sharing and caring? Could this also be a way they had of attacking what they feared? And a way of protecting against something they feared?

What is it that they feared?

What does that fear do to them?

Why do you imagine that they fear such things?

Then would you say that this problem-event became a model to teach you how to protect yourself against what they found fearful? If so, could it not be a way of demonstrating their caring?

Caring

If they showed they cared, then you know they cared. You also know what it took for them to reach that level of intensity.

If this is as much as they can feel, as much as they can experience, and as much as they can show, then, this must have been one of their great moments.

The Problematic Background: the Milieu

There is another kind of problem that plays a role in shaping the image we have of ourselves. We call it the milieu problem, the everyday way of being of our family/clan helps shape the image we have of ourselves. What we may take as normal or the characteristic way the family/clan functions can also contribute to our self-image. The view a family has of itself and those outside it has a force; the style of life they casually toss out often contains a shape within which they want members of the clan to conform. Political, religious, and social stereotypes become things to be or to avoid. These ways of being are the models we are expected to imitate. To the degree they limit and restrict us from expressing a more genuine and more rational way of being, they too need to be questioned and rejected.

These background influences have a strong influence without their having a particular origin in a pathologos drama, yet they too are problems to be dealt with. Pathologos problems affect early development while background influences affect latter development. Philosophers such as Plato describe these later influences as most detrimental to the child since they block a rational view of oneself and society. In Homer's *Iliad,* we can find examples of early pathologos shaping in the childhood of Achilles. The story shows the irrational forces that reduce man to a shadow of himself and that bring about the suffering of man. The narrative shows us that to truly to be a whole person is to go beyond race, religion, and custom.

This theme of being a truly rational being is dramatically present in Aeschylus' *Suppliant Maidens,* a magnificent tragedy well worth reading. Aristotle put it well when he said that being a Hellene, a Greek, has nothing to do with where you were born or the language you speak, but being what one truly is, a Man—a Person. Thus, becoming rational, we become a Hellene and celebrate the genuine life, including becoming a rational Self.

The Milieu You Face

Now it is important to contrast the way your family appeared during that problem-event with your impressions of them at other times.

Describe how each of those present in the problem-event normally appeared to you when they weren't in a problem.

How did they seem to you during those times?

If they were to act this way all the time, how would that affect you?

And, if that's the way they were all the time, how could you tell they cared about you or what you were doing?

Now, as you review the way they usually were, would you agree you could describe that way of being as if it were the background, or the stage setting, within which the problem scenes played themselves out?

By accepting this distinction, we can raise this question to a new level. What kinds of circumstances does it take for your problem to emerge and play itself out?

Predict when your problem will most likely play itself out.

And, now that you have examined it again, would you say that there are special times when the players in a problem can come out and show their feelings and express themselves and other times when they cannot?

But when are you most real?

When are you most purely your real self?

When do you become sincere even to yourself—and when not?

Consider another thing, how did your family drama play itself out while watching TV together, or when taking trips or vacations together, and during other family gatherings? Discuss whether or not exceptions were made during these times and the effect that had on you.

How did your family relate during the preparation of meals, during dinner, cleaning up after dinner and on weekends? How were the housecleaning chores used to play out the background of the family drama?

Roles in the Event

Therefore, as you consider the diagram of your past problem-event and the way each of the parties related to each other, can you also describe the way they behaved or functioned?

What role would you say each is playing?

Who do they seem most like as they act out their roles?

Can you recall any roles from literature, the movies, television, or mythology that are similar to those roles you described in the diagram?

Can you see when and how you play out similar roles in your life?

Can you tell, or distinguish, when you play this or that role?

Sometimes it may seem that some roles are better than others—but is it not likely that any role is an act and should be avoided?

However, if there is a family role you might like to play out, which one would it be? Why?

And who would get your old role? Why?

In what way does playing that role seem better than not playing any role at all?

Family Recollections

This section is to help you see what you have learned about the struggles the members of your family went through to achieve their goals.

Can you remember what those in your family have said about the sacrifices they made in order to achieve their goals?

What was their idea of work? How did they communicate to you what they felt about going to work, working, and leaving their work? What image of work did they have?

Can you also recall how they seemed to you when they spoke about these things?

What impressions were you gaining about life, about the meaning and significance of the sacrifices and the struggles they went through to achieve their goals?

Please add your reflections about your parents' recollections and interactions with their own parents, your grandparents, for you learned from them, too. Be watchful for the patterns which are becoming familiar to you.

Please add your recollection of how you saw your parents interacting with their own families.

Reflect on the stories your parents told about their own youth; what can you find that reflects your own problem?

To what extent can you see that a problem is handed down from one generation to another?

Consider, *you can stop this transmission in your lifetime*; there is no necessity for your children to inherit what you never wanted.

Time to Reflect

As we did earlier, we have supplied a chart outlining where in the process you are now, and where you are going from here. Please take some time to review this. It is our intent to help you understand this process and feel comfortable with proceeding. You have just finished Part Four.

Part One	A Goal and the Problem
Part Two	Revealing the Problem
Part Three	Uncovering the Past
Part Four	Reflecting on the Past
Part Five	**Questioning What Has Been Discovered**
Part Six	**Power of Silence and Power of Words**
Part Seven	**Knowing and Convincing**
Part Eight	**Taking the Challenge**
Part Nine	**Self Discovery**
Part Ten	**Higher Goals**

Part Five:

Questioning What Has Been Discovered

You have done a very good job reflecting and have faced and answered many probing questions, which certainly shows you are now ready to question the meaning of that past problem event.

Consider that for all this intensity and display of feelings which you have just described, you can still ask whether or not they were right in what they said and did.

Consider and ask yourself seriously if you see something about what was going on that you could question.

Being Fair

As you reflect on this past problem-event, could you say that the participants were fair in what they said and did? You know—you were there.

Was their exceptional behavior justified?

In what way(s) were they trying to show you or convince you about something that was important to them? And yet, you are now seeing you actually had reason to reject that very thing that was happening right there in front of you.

In what way could you say they were wrong?

Doubts

As you proceed through this workbook, you may wonder if the event happened in the way you have recalled it, and you may be concerned whether you are being fair or not in the way you have represented those in the past event.

Motives

You may even doubt your motives and question what you have said, but you will find that these concerns, while legitimate, are not *as* significant when compared with understanding just why you are presently thinking in this way. Indeed, you may change your account of this and other events as often as you deem necessary, and for each version, you will learn something that is significant.

The Prism

You will discover that each time you return to these early events, you will find in them new ways of understanding your present and past, for a problem is much like having a many faceted prism whose sides reflect slightly different views, each having its own valuable mode of perceiving a level of truth. These levels are eminently worth seeing.

The Justification

At this point in your exploration, you have seen the effect your youthful conclusions have made on your life.

As you consider the many occasions in your early life when your problem played itself out, can you say what its origin was? Can you say WHAT or WHO often started if off?

Would you say that those responsible for the problem felt they were justified in doing what they did?

If this is so, would it not be that some member of the family, or an authority, felt justified in taking some course of action against you, or others? And what was their justification?

Indeed, if there was some reason that generated the problem, is it not likely that it was some kind of violation of one of your family's laws, or some rule of the house that was challenged? Please explain what law, or principle, was violated in your case.

In other circumstances, you could have witnessed an event in which you played a minor role—and yet no family law or rule was necessarily broken; however, you may have felt it was a basic violation of what was right or fair. In either case, would you agree that those who play a role in the problem-event suffer from some sense of injustice having been done either to them, or to another? Please describe that injustice.

And is there not some feeling that when one is a witness to injustice there must be some act of vindication or revenge to make things just and so resolve the injustice? Please explain.

And then, if it cannot be resolved, it is left undone and it remains on our mind. And so, what do we do?

.....We promise ourselves we will deal with the insult at some later time and so, for the time being, we brood, plan, and suffer in silence.

The Secret

Is not this sense of being justified in what you say and do an intense state of mind?

Consider your own past; recall those who appeared self-righteous, those who felt justified in their actions, and those who appeared to suffer as martyrs. Are not these the high and intense moments when you learned what mattered most to these people?

Clearly, this was a moment that lifted those concerned into a role that raised them above their everyday lifestyles or mode of being. Were not these moments among the most intense that you have ever seen these people in? Please explain what you think about this in some detail.

While the problem was unfolding through each of its scenes, were you not witnessing the disclosure of something that mattered most to the actors in this drama?

Were you seeing what they considered most significant to them—something they did not share with everyone? Something you could regard as either a secret or something they preferred to keep to themselves?

Before you shared in this secret, there must have been many things that were unclear to you, and now, since it was shared with you and you are part of it, wasn't much of what was previously confusing made clear?

How did you become a party to it? Could it be that since you didn't oppose it, your silence assured them that you accepted it? Or at least that you wouldn't oppose it?

And does it seem to you that it is binding upon you until you express your disapproval to them by putting that disapproval into words? Please explain.

But what do you think; would your expressed opposition to them and what went on during that problem-event risk your exile from the group?

Are you coming to the idea that family problems produce clan membership? If so, does that mean that problems are what keep us primitive-members of clan beliefs?

Could It All have Been Avoided?

On the other hand, wouldn't all of this have changed if those in command had inquired into the reasons why someone in the house appeared to be withdrawn and suffering, or why the laws and rules of the family had been broken?

Or, if that wouldn't have changed anything, what could have?

Is it not likely that if some authority had sought to understand the circumstances of the situation, rather than reacting to it, that it would have changed things so much that the problem would not have come into existence?

But if it were possible for that understanding to have developed, wouldn't that mean that those involved would have moved from merely being members of a clan to becoming members of a real family, or group? Please explain.

The Mask

Have these past problem-events changed you in some important way? Because, if you have changed, then understanding such a change could tell you much about your present condition as well as indicate your future development.

Let us consider this in some detail: First, reflect on the past problem and note carefully the different states of mind that you experienced in each scene. Include, as well, the way you were functioning, or doing what you were doing.

As you reflect on these past problem scenes, would you agree that you were led to certain conclusions, or views, about your reality and yourself? What would you say they were? How do you imagine those views shaped your vision of the world? Of men? Of women? And of relationships?

Then, before that past problem-event you didn't have those views, and to that degree you were different, were you not? Compare the views you had before and after; what do you see?

Again, is it possible that the past problem-event would not have entered its first scene were it not that you were revealing a positive state of mind? Were you not actually in a GOOD state of mind? Is it possible that you were revealing a positive state of mind just before the problem was acted out? Consider and try to describe the state of mind that you were in before the problem "came down" upon you.

Why did the drama of the problem and its lesson come down so heavily when you were in that state of mind?

After the problem-event played itself out, what happened to that state of mind that you were in prior to the drama that took place?

Have you ever been able to be as you were then, initially, and to manifest that positive state of mind again?

Did the unfolding drama of that problem end the appearance of that state of mind? Did it stop you from revealing that state of mind?

If you were in a better state of mind before the problem acted itself out, then what is the meaning of that loss? By the way, had you forgotten until now that you were in a better state of mind before that event?

Through that problem-event, did you learn something that kept you from showing that state of mind again? Please explain.

Was this scene the origin of your identifying with another state of mind—one that was not and is not your own?

Is this when you picked up your problem and learned to act like someone else?

How do you understand this curious transformation? Do you see that by identifying with another you became less than you were—and therefore, not fully yourself?

If this is so, must you not reclaim your past to become fully yourself and must you not leave behind your identification with another's role, or game, to proceed with your development?

Even today, would you not like to return to that state of mind and be as you were prior to that problem-event? If so, then your future development depends on going back and recovering what you left behind, doesn't it?

Part Six:
Power of Silence and Power of Words

Silence

Let us reflect together for a moment or two about the role of silence.

First, please recall a past situation when, even though you wanted to, you didn't speak your mind as you would have liked.

Can you recall what state of mind that silence put you into and then, what you said to yourself?

Now, see if you can recall exactly what you said to yourself; since this might be difficult, please recall a recent event when you didn't express yourself over some injustice, perhaps over something you heard about or saw. What was that moment like? Please describe it.

Then, as you consider the impact of such scenes, could you describe what you believe it would be like if this state became more intense?

What name would you give to this state of mind?

What is IT?

Since you have just described that state of mind, would you say it is like some kind of annoyance?

Or perhaps some kind of frustration?

And what is behind this feeling? Is it anger?

Do you get angry at some people but not others? Do those you get angry at seem to keep you from expressing yourself?

Are you waiting for them to change before you express yourself? Does waiting for them to change keep you irritated and silent?

But consider, are you angry with yourself for being silent?

Returning to Our Questioning

What state of mind would you say this kind of "silence" puts you into?

What do you believe it would be like to break your silence and put into words what you see about what most concerns you?

What would you be freeing by putting an end to your anger?

And If...

And if you keep the anger—preserving it and even nourishing it— then how is that related to silence, to the role you have learned to play, and to the struggle to free yourself from the beliefs that you have created from your past? What if whatever you don't take exception to, or speak out against, feeds your fantasy life? For there you can play out the drama again and again, arguing against what you can't oppose in your waking life.

Keeping Silent

Consider: to be silent and to say nothing of what you see, keeps silent what you see. To keep that silent about what you see silences yourself and keeps you convinced that you are unable to risk saying what you see.

But you did come to a conclusion about what went on, only you never put it into words, so it lives on as an attitude or a feeling which has shaped and molded your very personality. "Putting it into words" surfaces what you have kept silent, even from yourself.

Why is the idea of sacrificing what you see connected with the appearance of caring and love?

Putting it into Words

Reflecting on this past problem-event, what do you imagine you would like to have said to those who were present?

As you consider expressing that point of view, is it possible that you could add to it so that it does justice to everything you have been reflecting upon?

YOU CAN SAY IT

You! You are a man! You have a VOICE...speak your mind, for meaningful sounds have been awaited since immeasurable time. Give voice to the vision of Man. And through continual questioning and reflection may you polish to a brilliance that which illuminates the soul, and so, ends the dark silence of the ages.

....Words

What effect do you think this would have had on each of those present?

What effect would it have had on the members of your family?

How would that have affected your relationships with them?

Had they discussed these problems scenes the day after they occurred, so that each person could express what they felt and saw, do you think that would have changed things?

Why do you think so?

Would discussing these things, either at the time or later, have changed the way you and others could relate to one another?

If you and the others had discussed this matter, in what way would your relationship have changed?

Then why wasn't it discussed?

If so much could change with so little effort, why wasn't it done?

Do you think it might still have an effect to discuss these things, if not with them with someone else?

Now... What do you think of that?

Part Seven:
Knowing and Convincing

Now consider another thing: in respect to those people in these early problem-events that you have described, in what way would you say they appeared most real and sincere in what they said and did during that event?

At the time when they appeared that sincere, would you say that they presented themselves as confident and knowing? Did they seem more sure, more confident, and more knowing than at other times? Please explain.

But for all their acting and appearing, were they, at that time, really knowing? Is it not possible that they themselves have been convinced that appearing in that way is what it means to be a knower?

Will you please describe the times when you, too, use that way of appearing in your relations with others? Please explain.

Or, on the other hand, in order to avoid appearing *as* any kind of knower, have you kept your own level of knowing incomplete? What does that mean?

Would you say that you have waited for scenes similar to that past scene before you allow the appearance of "the knower" within you to emerge? Please explain.

Review those scenes in your life when you play a "knower," trying to convince someone that you are right....or justified.

Is there a way of playing "dumb" or stupid at other times?

Please describe what it is like when you don't reveal the full content of what you know even though the situation requires it.

How will your life change if you decide to drop appearing as a "knower" or a "dope" during such scenes?

But if this "appearing as a knower" that comes from the problem scene is NOT knowing, then what is? And how should you appear as a "knower" if you do know? And without this appearance of knowing, how will others know when you want to be known as a knower?

Consider the past scene you are exploring once more, because you have seen how the role of the knower plays an important part in the past drama; contrast that way of appearing with the time when you were most sincerely, truly knowing?

Were you able to be most yourself in that moment when you revealed your knowing?

And, in that moment, was there any trace of an attitude that was unnecessary? What would it mean if you recognize some mask or attitude when you present your knowing?

In what way is revealing yourself as a knower connected with showing someone that you care about them?

Please describe a few scenes in your life when you experienced this kind of knowing and caring. Would you explain in what way these scenes could be described as showing love?

Are showing love and knowing related? Compare the scenes when you would say someone showed love and caring and then contrast them with the knowing scenes. How do they differ? Explain.

As you consider the past scenes from which your problems emerged, would you say that in each and every one that there is someone who is playing a "knower" and showing they care? Does the caring reveal knowing, or does knowing show caring?

Must both be present? And does this create the impression that love is present? And, in that moment when knowing and caring both seem to be present, is this the very occasion for the transmission of belief?

Reflect further on this very insightful moment and consider the way the players in your drama appeared. They were revealing themselves, were they not? And in this moment, would you say that there was a certain kind of beauty present, in spite of all that may have happened in those scenes? In what way can you say that you encountered a certain kind of beauty?

Now, drawing from your own reflections and experiences of your own problems, please explain what you think was the effect upon you of encountering the appearance of love, knowing, caring, beauty and belief? Please put into your own words what you would say that this means.

Part Eight:
Taking the Challenge

Do you have a problem because you feel inferior, or do you feel inferior because you believe something about yourself that makes you feel inferior?

Surely there may have been times when it seemed to you that you were inferior because you were in a problem. But is there a particular reason, or teaching, you have accepted about yourself that has bred that feeling of inferiority?

If we can't stop applying the wrong solution from the past to a present situation, does it suggest that we must be irrational or bad, or worse?

Again, let us put the question in another form: Why do we apply past solutions to the present? Is it because we can't help it? Are we irrational if we can't stop ourselves from applying the same faulty solutions to our present problems?

Consider your past scenes once again and ask yourself whether or not it seems that those present had reached a limit that they couldn't be expected to go beyond? What leads you to believe that they couldn't go beyond that way of appearing?

But consider the past problem scenes and ask yourself in what way your handling of your problem avoided an even greater confrontation?

Is it likely that if you had challenged them even further than you did, that it would have made the situation worse than it was?

But, given the forces in your problem-scenes, can you say you were defeated, or did you actually find a way to survive?

Well, you survived!

You made it through your early years and found a way to adapt to those around you.

You needed to adapt because you depended upon them for your subsistence, and so you remained silent and, perhaps, nursed a grievance from that point on.

Consider, are the lessons you learned from those past scenes your failures, or your partial successes?

Could it be that the problem you are now having in your life is simply a case where you are applying a past solution to a present situation because it seems so similar to the past, so that you act it out somewhat automatically and just naturally expect that the old solution will work?

Rather than conclude before giving yourself an opportunity to reflect on your experience, ask yourself if you always have doubts or reservations about yourself when you are in situations in which you are likely to confront your problem.

Or do you act spontaneously without any kind of reflection, without any recollection of having confronted similar situations in the past?

Please reflect on your recent experiences when you consider these questions. Do you allow yourself to play out the problem?

Do you just go along with it, taking no stand in respect to what's going on?

Well, what state of mind are you in when you recognize that you may, once more, resume an old pattern that you would prefer to avoid?

But, to oppose what is going on, to take a position against the flow of events taking place, what does that take?

Would it take a decision from you to take a stand? What kind of decision would that be? What would you be leaving and what would you be moving towards?

What do you think it will be like to encounter your problem and look at it directly, to see it for what it is, and then to see if you can be true to yourself and be what you most want to be?

And would taking such a stand be exhibiting the courage to be rational?

But you can ignore all this and return to playing out the dramas of your problem, can't you?

Or can you knowingly act against what you know? And what you see?

Is it possible that you have already seen too much to play out the old problem games in the old way?

Surprised

Yet aren't you often surprised when you recall that the solutions offered by your problem only work in one place, that they have the full effect only in one place, and that they are only understood in one place?

Are your solutions acceptable only at home? Is the only place where they are accepted either at home, or a place that tolerates the same drama?

Time to Reflect

Before moving on we have again outlined where you have been and where we are going next in this process. Please take the time to review and reflect on this process and your strides within it. You have just finished Part Eight.

Part One	A Goal and the Problem
Part Two	Revealing the Problem
Part Three	Uncovering the Past
Part Four	Reflecting on the Past
Part Five	Questioning What Has Been Discovered
Part Six	Power of Silence and Power of Words
Part Seven	Knowing and Convincing
Part Eight	Taking the Challenge
Part Nine	**Self Discovery**
Part Ten	**Higher Goals**

Part Nine:
Self Discovery

The Fear of Understanding and Emptiness

Consider for a moment the positive features of your problem and those who play a vital role in it. It is actually a world-view, it is a family inheritance from the remote past, it is has been carried along for generations and has fallen into your lap.

It made a bond among believers, it formed a way of being that is immediately recognized and brings acceptance to those who accept it.

To reject it may bring an experience of freedom, but it also deprives you, at least to some degree, of membership in that clan belief.

As you experience this you will notice a fear creeps in. A fear that has a haunting refrain, "Now, what will you do without those beliefs that have chained you?" Can you dare stand alone and live without what had formerly created a safety net for you to live within?

Yes, this fear is natural; this fear has been nurtured in every way by those who live within that realm of belief.

However, do you not see everywhere that there are people who can be free in sports or in music and are not bound by these restricting beliefs? They have reached a degree of freedom and spontaneity. They can act quite appropriately to the circumstances they find themselves in, without these chains of belief that limit their vision and life. However, it is often the case that when they leave that arena they step back into their old way of being.

Now comment on this; reflect on your own experience and write down in your journal your thoughts and feeling about this fear of the mind and understanding.

Consider what it would be like for you to discuss this issue with your family and friends. What reaction do you think you might encounter? What could you say in response?

Reflection

What would you think if you were getting insights into your problem and then found that you were functioning better than you had been before, would you still think that the origin of your problem is that you are intrinsically bad, inferior or flawed?

What does that mean? Does that mean that your parents, or the family, are responsible for your suffering?

Does the need to achieve personal excellence require that you abandon your family and all parental authority? Should you not be bold enough to face this issue?

Self

What are we? Consider: you have seen how your problem manifests itself in your present and past circumstances and how it may affect your future. We need to explore and review the relationship between our problems and our self, so let us reflect together and ask:

What are we? Are we only these problems and nothing else?

Stripped of these problems, might we discover that we are nothing?

At least when we were ignorant of our problems, we thought we were something, but now what image or role can we say we have?

Don't our problems give us a direction, a way of appearing, a way of relating with others, and most importantly, a way to love and be loved?

Sure, we might say a part of our former life was a fiction, or an illusion, but still it gave us a sense of being something and if that were stripped away, wouldn't we feel that we must face this world without that something that gave us, at least in some measure, our identity?

If you keep peeling away the layers of belief, is it possible we may end up as nothing? Is this what we must face? Why?

Is that sense of nothingness simply the effect of losing a role you no longer have to play, or a mask or image you will no longer have to present?

Could that sense of nothingness mask your anger and resentment?

And is it possible that as long as the anger and resentment remain silent, you will remain bound to that role and image?

If so, what do you imagine it would be like to express yourself to people who are important to you without the masks and roles that support some image of yourself?

Self: The Moment of Decision

When you think about expressing yourself at those times without either that old image or role, it may seem that you will need a kind of courage as well as a sense of fairness, and you may feel you lack these qualities.

Further, it may be argued that without these qualities, we may be stuck in a morass of indecision, unable to emerge from our problem; but to say that, of course, merely delays the moment of confronting and testing our problem, doesn't it? So, then, what is there in that moment that we are often reluctant to face?

Self: Freedom and Understanding

When we leave these old belief structures behind us, and act without their images and roles, it is then that we are no longer being influenced by false beliefs about ourselves. It is then that we can reach towards an understanding that is richer and more humane than we could have experienced before. It is the time for growing into freedom and integrity.

Risking

It may seem that it requires risk to make this transition, but it doesn't. It may seem that it should require the development of those moral qualities, but it doesn't. It merely requires that you decide to act in terms of your own vision. But a voice declares that if we act with such spontaneity we might be wrong, we might make a mistake.

Yes, that's true. You might make a mistake, but how else are we best to test our vision? How else are we to discover that higher knowing which only comes when we risk making mistakes?

Reflecting on Insights

Now it is time to reflect together on some insights you have gained concerning the roots of your problem. You have seen that many of your personal difficulties have their origins in your early struggle to reach maturity.

With this new awakening, a kinship with the mind brings to an end what we call *the fear of the mind.* It is with this freedom that we play a conscious role in our destiny.

Ignorance

Consider the sacrifices—far too numerous to mention—that your parents have made for you, and reflect on the fact that your very existence depended upon their efforts. Thus, when they revealed to you what was most central to them, were they not revealing the beliefs that formed the core of their own thought? But do you think they knew whether those beliefs were true or not?

Were they not passing on to you what had been passed on to them? Were they not passing on things that they may have believed only for that moment and which served the needs of only that moment?

And could it be that they didn't even know why they were saying and doing such things? And if they were asked why they did what they did, is it not likely that they would not have a good answer?

If they had known the consequences that event would have on your life, is it not likely that they would have gladly avoided those early scenes?

And now that you see the consequences of your problems on your life, how will you avoid them?

Our Inheritance

What these explorations reveal again and again is that those who have created the conditions for our problems did not know the effect it would have on us. Had they known, they would never have acted out that pattern. Remember that they too were victims of the very same problem they introduced to you—for they were following a pattern they didn't understand any more than you when you "do to others what they once did to you."

Relationships and Understanding

How would your relationships proceed if you were to bring to them a better understanding of yourself?

And what of love? Could your relationships and love mature and be expressions of your own inner development?

But don't you agree that development, as a process, goes through stages? And so, what may be appropriate for one stage may not be appropriate for another?

What is a Problem?

Let us reflect together once more and consider an alternative view.

Could a problem be a sin?

Are there times when you believe you are suffering because you have done something bad?

Is it possible that the root cause of your problem is simply and solely the result of something like pride, arrogance, and emotions overcoming you?

On the other hand, do you believe you are overcome with such things as pride and arrogance because you are bad?

Consider, shouldn't there be a reason for the manifestation of things as pride and arrogance? And even for being bad?

In what way does judging what you have done as something bad help you understand what you have done?

And, even if you do judge yourself as either good or bad, can that be an explanation of your present and past? Isn't an explanation finding reasons for why we do what we do?

In what way do you think that you would benefit by discovering why you do what you do? If you were to discover those reasons that would explain "why you do what you do," how would that help you deal with your present life?

Consider, if you can benefit by understanding your problem, then should you not expect your everyday experience to provide you with opportunities for you to learn and understand yourself?

And, if understanding matures your vision, in what way would that lead you to reflect upon your higher good? And on your higher goals? What do you think about this?

Conditions for a Problem

If you understand the nature of a problem—yours or anyone else's—then you will have a clear idea of why it was necessary for it to manifest when and how it did.

When you understand the conditions for the existence of a problem, you will also understand that what you have learned, you use, and that what you do not oppose, you allow.

We apply past solutions—or learnings—to circumstances that are similar. What blocked us in the past blocks us in the present.

Do you have any idea why your problem should have arisen when it did? Why at that moment, or time, rather than another?

Given what you have seen, does this mean that your present problems should arise when they do?

Then, does that mean there is a logic to problems and a reason for their existence?

Why would it be "just" for you to have the problem you have, and "just" for you to live without problems?

Why Must It Change?

If you were to grow out of your problem, would that not include leaving both your problem and the background of normality you previously described? And do you not experience those two primary states of mind either while being in your problem, or in the background of normality?

Are they merely two sides of the same coin? Does the problem state include both acting out the problem and then waiting for the parts of the problem to come together again? In what way does it seem to you that the background of normality, the milieu, has a dark cloud hanging over it?

What would it be like to eliminate, or resolve, your problem and to leave that background of normality, the milieu, untouched? Would you settle for that? WHY?

Does the possibility of the drama of the game extending itself into the background of your own life deprive it of something significant to you? In what way?

Reclaiming the Past

Consider this question: Do you have problems because certain past events happened to you—or is the origin of your problems found in the conclusions you made regarding those past events?

And further, did those conclusions you made distort your understanding of the event itself?

Now that you have reached a different way of understanding your past, how does that change your view of those past problem scenes?

Again, did you have an accurate view of your past if it was distorted by the conclusions you made?

Consider. Could it be that to the degree you challenge those distortions, to that very degree you have a memory of the past, a past that is more accurate than before? But if that is so, wouldn't it mean that you are not merely gaining a way to eliminate problems, but also a way to reclaim your past?

Can you say then, to the very degree you have problems, to that very degree you have a distorted past?

And could you say that having a problem means having a distorted past—or a past that has been heavily interpreted?

Consider. If you have recalled interpretations of those past scenes and not your past, what would it be like to recall a past without interpreting it? What does that mean?

Speculations on the Pathologos

And now it is time to speculate on your reflections and then, later, we will use this exploration to ponder the closing questions.

But first, do you agree you have seen how the beliefs you came to, about the meaning of important events in your life, are the origin of your problems?

Consider, would you say that in your own life you have seen enough to say that accepting a pathologos serves to bind and preserve the family, clan, religious or social group's closeness or unity?

And does it preserve the role of authority?

Does accepting that belief make it more difficult for members to leave the group and separate themselves from that pathologos' influence?

Does the transmission of the pathologos occur when members challenge or threaten the group's belief structure? Does this often occur when the members are young and dependent upon the group for their survival?

And did those who convinced you of the "truth" of the pathologos do so by appearing so believable that any rejection of it would also have meant rejecting the way they appeared?

But wasn't that the time when those you loved appeared most knowing, most caring, most intense, most beautiful, and most powerful?

And wasn't that the time when they revealed what they thought and felt about you?

Surely, that was the time that they seemed to share themselves with you, so that moment is important to you. It provides a model of love, recognition, and knowing, doesn't it?

Were you not in a bind then? How can you reject that pathologos without rejecting them? How could you have called the message false without calling the medium false?

Could you take exception to such beliefs? Could you discuss it openly with all members to see if an alternative could be found? Then why didn't you?

Is your silence accepted as evidence that you will not oppose that belief, so that any actions proceeding from it will not be challenged?

Does your silence fix you within the bounds of the problem's structure? Does it mean you support what you do not oppose? Why?

Can you recognize and accept your own anger? Can you see it when you face your own silence? Would putting it into words end the silence and the anger? Why?

Do you find something common in all those scenes that you encountered—in that silence and anger?

Do you find that you are drawn to scenes that are similar to your past scene, analogous to it, and so you play out your role over and over?

Does the acceptance of the pathologos set the limits of your growth and block your maturity?

But doesn't it also present you with the opportunity for growth? For consider what you have seen for a moment. Perhaps whatever happened in that past problem-event was actually a reflection of the highest wisdom available to those present. Now if you can hold on to this possibility and assume it for the moment, then, considering this: what, ideally, should you have said and done?

If you had dealt with that past problem-event on the most ideal level, what impact do you suppose it would have had on your present problem? What do you suppose you should have said during that past problem-event? What does this mean, then?

The Questions

Now that you have proceeded step by step through these questions, you have reached many conclusions, some of which are likely to be firm and secure while others may be tentative, but, in either case, now we should review them and bring them together into a unity.

What would you say is the origin and the cause of much of the suffering and anguish in your life?

How is this suffering related to the obstacles you encountered in pursuit of your goals?

How does resolving problems remove the obstacles to achieving personal excellence?

To what degree would you say that others may reach similar conclusions to these questions?

Does that mean you have reached a new view of how mankind has been molded and shaped by the pressures of family, clan, society and religion?

Well, then what is your view of being human and of yourself? If a person can be freed from these pressures, what do you think might be the proper destiny of such a person?

What path is open for a person to explore the depths of his being?

The Inter-Relationships of Problems

As you experience other obstacles in the pursuit of your goals, you can return to this workbook and explore each of them as you just did with your current problem.

After you have used this workbook on several of your problems, you may begin to see their interrelationships. When you compare what you have learned from each of your problems, you will discover that they can be linked together and that they form the content of your underlying belief structure.

The full content of your problem becomes visible when you have seen how all of the conclusions fit together; they mutually support one another and make up your fundamental beliefs about yourself and your reality. Quite naturally the connections you discover will bring about insights regarding many of your prior conclusions, and add greater precision to them, as well as giving them greater scope. It is in seeing their inter-relationships and what they support that you can free yourself from their influence.

If you review the diagrams of your present problem events, and observe how they too can be linked together, your analysis can proceed with more precision. First notice how similar states of mind appear in more than one of your diagrams and from that common feature, you can begin to connect them together.

Now, do the same thing with those diagrams from your past and find how they can be inter-related. You will find that some of them seem to fit together and you will understand how they are inter-related. You will find that some of them seem to fit into clusters and others seem to have a life of their own; but on closer inspection you can discover the bridge that links them together, creating a powerful and dynamic virus whose contamination spreads through generations, sabotaging its victims highest aspirations and confining them to dwell among the shadows of false beliefs.

Bringing it all Together

Again, you should review the diagrams and identify the masks you have worn, when you have used them and the consequences of wearing them. Describe them and find models or pictures of them. Catalogue them. Watch for their appearance in your daily life so that you can add more details to these descriptions.

Become aware of key terms in your explorations—especially those slogans that pass for truths and enshrine family sayings—and become attentive to the context in which they occur during your explorations. You can easily identify some of them by paying attention to the language used when you recalled what was said in those past scenes that you diagrammed.

Notice how those key terms play a major role in your life, in your fantasy life, and in your actions. Review past pages to see the places and circumstances where you used these key ideas while going through the workbook. By studying when and where they appear, you can see the role they are playing in your thought processes.

Each time you use this analysis to explore your problems, you will be seeing another aspect of it that you hadn't seen before. By returning and subjecting your beliefs to analysis, you will be solving your problems. By seeing each aspect of your problem and the relationship to each of its other aspects, and then by testing your vision, you will be allowing an intellectual functioning which develops an understanding that grows richer as it frees itself of entangling false beliefs.

Consider another thing. Will you not have diminished, or ended, in your own lifetime, the effect of false beliefs that have blocked your growth and development? Have you not also done much to put an end to a way of being—a tradition that has caused innumerable sacrifices to be made to something that no one understood?

Having completed this journey, you are to be congratulated for answering these questions sincerely. Reflecting on the self is, of course, a time-honored path into self-discovery and personal growth; it is an ongoing process, a part of that noblest game, Philosophical Midwifery. Your continual reflection upon your life is a perfecting process that brings the luster of excellence to the self.

Reflection

"...But one thing I would fight for to the end, both in word and deed if I were able - that if we believed that we must try to find out 'what is not known,' we should be better and braver and less idle than if we believed that 'what we do not know' is impossible to find out and that we need not even try."

Plato, *Meno*

Part Ten:
Higher Goals

You have taken a profound journey and have gone through much trouble and travail, but you have returned home. What you have gone through is very similar to what Achilles did in Homer's *Iliad*. There you will find the archetype, the model, of self-discovery. Achilles was the worst of men but he faced his problem and saw its depth. He discovered the forces that bound him and it is very similar to what you have experienced.

The second journey of the soul is Odysseus' return home to Ithaka, the goal of Homer's *Odyssey*. Now, with your new state of mind and the challenge to be yourself without compromise you need to show yourself before significant others. This is our second journey. For the self that has seen through its problems can now speak and be with a clarity and purity.

Thus, we invite you to an act of imagination. We will start a story and you finish it. Add to it everything that comes to your mind. If any conflicts emerge please address each of them and continue on. Find yourself a comfortable place, alone and reflective, and imagine the following:

> *You have returned to your family and friends and they are having a banquet. You enter and you describe that you have resumed an early interest that you had abandoned and are now enjoying it. You say this struggle you are going through to master this activity has sharpened your interest in bringing an excellence to your everyday life, and they.....*

Good, now finish the daydream. See it vividly and see what you can learn. Whatever emerges that blocks you from being most fully yourself, just deal with it as a problem. Take yourself through this method of Philosophical Midwifery and bring to birth what needs to be begotten. But, in the daydream, do it in front of those who are present.

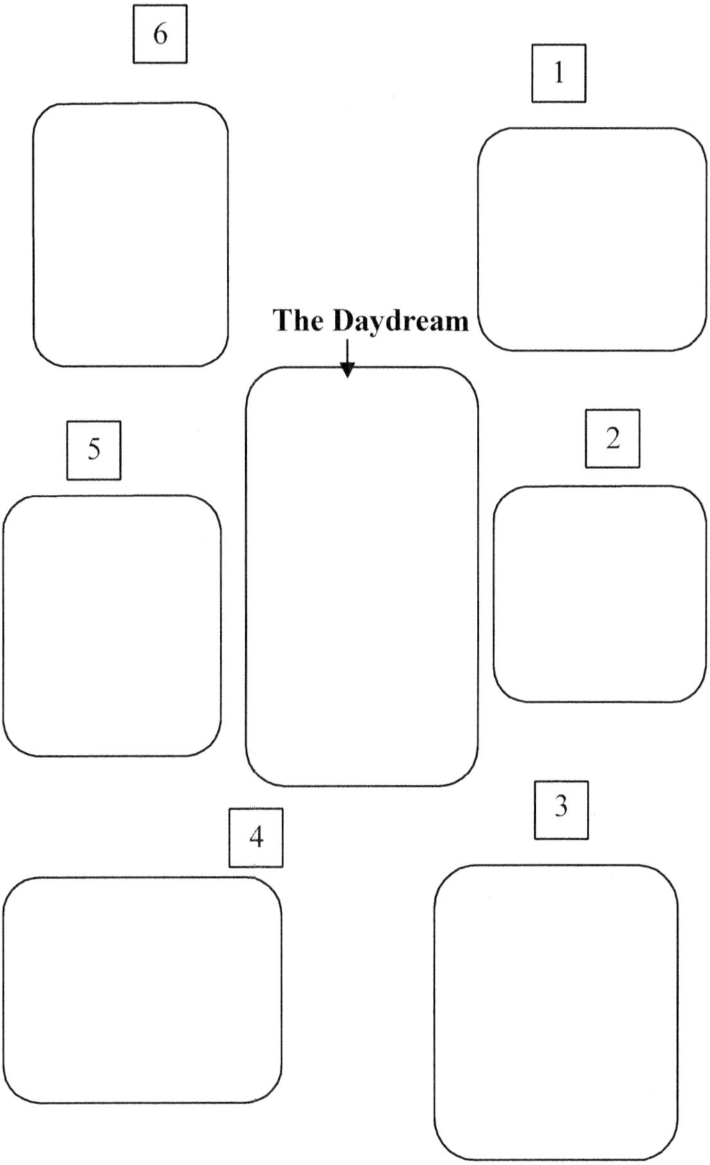
6
1
The Daydream
5
2
4
3

One more...

Follow the same instructions:

> *Now, you find yourself among some people you consider to be very profound. They are known for their insight and deep understanding of human nature and they enjoy one another's company. As they engage with one another they see you and invite you to join them. The oldest and wisest among them says, "Please sit here and tell us what is it that you have found about this mystery of existence that we are all a part of." You smile and thank them and begin, saying……*

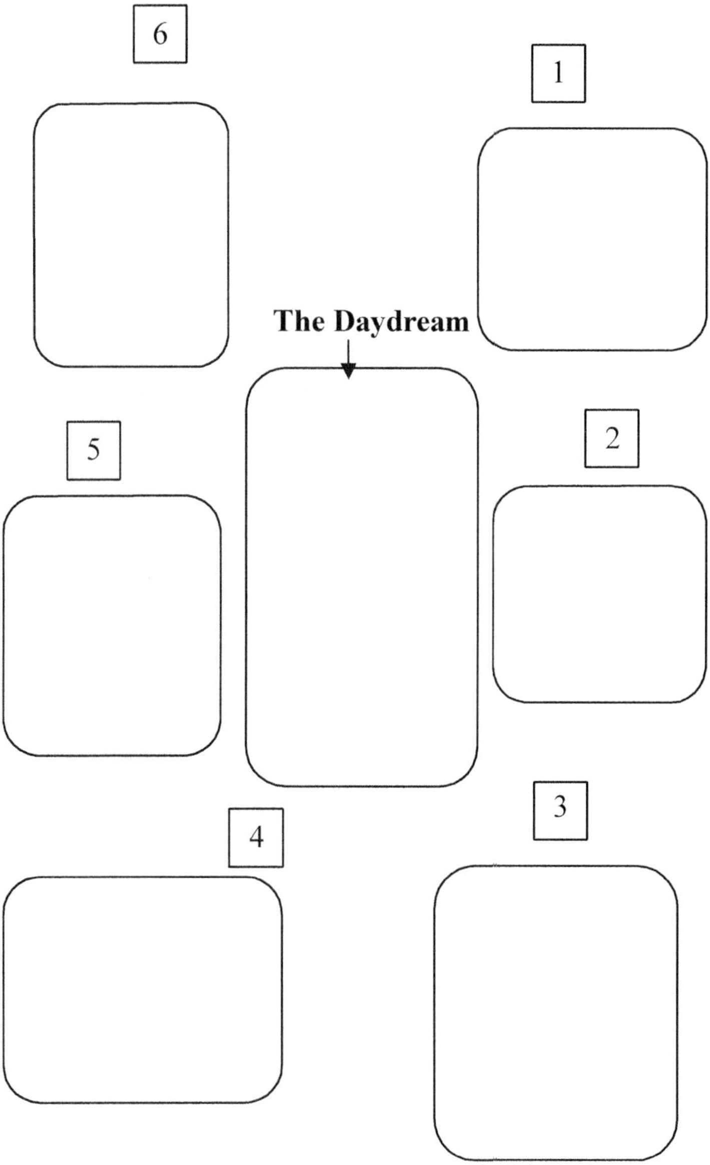
6
1
The Daydream
5
2
4
3

The Last Reflection

Now, reflect upon the meaning of what you have gone through, for, your future is in the palm of your hands.

And, now you can ask, "What is it that wants to Know?"

You have made a journey into understanding and have learned what it is like to see how things function and judge things in terms of the way they function.

Now, you can "go for broke." What is it you most would like to understand and come to know?

What major obstacles in your life would you like to overcome?

What is it that you most like to test yourself in mastering? What works or projects have you set aside that you can now enter into and seek to master? What will it be?

How about the great works of literature, Plotinus....Plato....Homer...Tolstoy?

What works are designed to challenge us most profoundly? Give it a try and watch a new class of problems emerge that you are now able to deal with.

So? Well, "go for broke!" Do it.

Why We Are Here

Whatever you say,
you know you said it.
Knowing you said it
makes you different
than before you said it
because
having put it into words,
you risked being wrong,
but you expressed it.
Now you understand
what you said and
you are shaped by what you said.
For you see through
your understanding like
you speak through your words, and
that becomes a way of being yourself.
So, express what is within you and
share what you see,
for we are here to see and to share what we see.

For more information about Pierre Grimes, visit the following websites:

www.academyofplatonicstudies.com
www.noeticsociety.org
www.openingmind.com
www.openingmind.net

Also see the bibliography section at the end of *The Pocket Pierre* by Pierre Grimes with Cathy Wilson.

Printed in Great Britain
by Amazon

82133884R00108